This book belongs to

_____

_____

Merry Christmas

COLOR TEST

SANTA MAZE

Help Santa Deliver the presents!

GINGERBREAD MAN GRAPHING

Count each Christmas picture, then graph it by coloring in the box every time you see it's picture.

🎁							
🍬							
🎄							
🧤							
🧥							

Christmas words

Fill in the missing letters

_IF_S

C_M_T

A_VE_T
_AL_ND_R

_O_K_ES

PE_GU_N

N__IV_TY
CEN

E___S

_NO_ G_O_E

_HO_OL_TE

GL_V_S

_IR_P_A_E

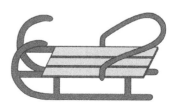

SL_DD_N_

CHRISTMAS

Complete the dot to dot to reveal the Christmas image. Color once completed.

Christmas COUNTING

Instructions: How many of each shape? Colour the images and write the total of each shape in the grid below:

FIND THE SHADOW!

Draw a line from the object to the correct shadow.

Santa's
sleigh

COUNT AND COLOR

Count the objects and color the correct number.

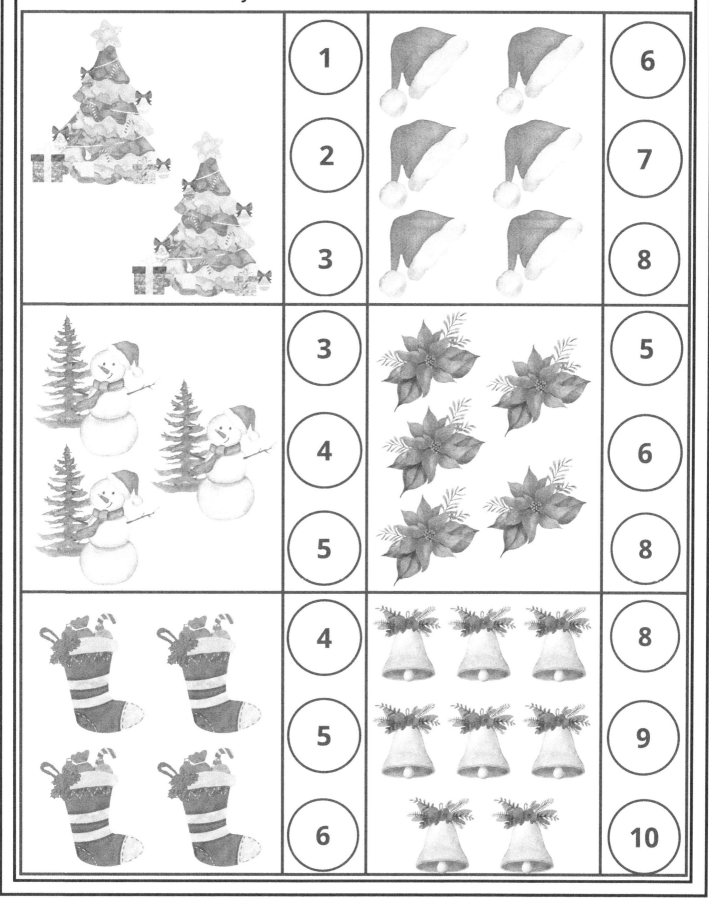

Holiday
WORD SEARCH

```
H D M D Y Y K S E V S A A S I
Y I G E J X J R D A G D T L C
D O T U R K E Y M R B N N E D
N P R E S E N T S C A Q A I J
A Z O A D B S N C M A C S G O
C Q L N Z I A A W O S R W H L
W A I D R T N O M Y T Y O Q L
V E N H I D N Q H E O I A L Y
R E C V L S G K W T C T N Z S
B W I E S N E C N I K N A R F
J T S T D D K H U A I U L B I
Y N B N R C D R V N B E L D
M I S T L E T O E R G E G M Z
U Z G Q W T E M T X Y V N C T
E K A C T I U R F A A M A D T
```

ANGEL	CANDLES	CANDY	CARDS
CAROLS	CHRISTMAS	FRANKINCENSE	FRUITCAKE
JOLLY	MISTLETOE	MYRRH	NATIVITY
PRESENTS	REINDEER	SANTA	SLEIGH
SNOWMAN	STOCKING	TREE	TURKEY

I Spy Christmas

Count the Christmas-themed items in the box and record the sum in the spaces provided below.

SWEET ADDITIONS

Find the sum in each equation.
Write your answer after the equal sign.

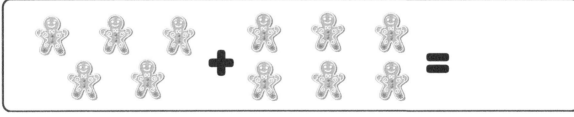

CHRISTMAS CODING

Examine the numbers corresponding to the Christmas cookies. Encode the passwords inside the circle with lines.

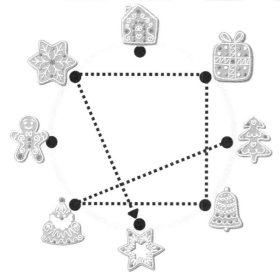

PASSWORD: 3-6-4-2-8-5

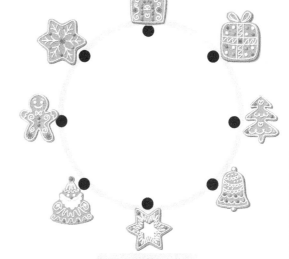

PASSWORD: 2-6-3-5-1-8

PASSWORD: 3-5-2-4-6-1

PASSWORD: 4-5-8-7-2-3

Find the Differences - Christmas

Can you find 5 differences in these two pictures?

Santa's reindeer

CHRISTMAS SUDOKU

Each row across and column down needs one of each image.
There can't be more than one image in any row across or column down.
Cut the pictures and paste them to complete Sudoku.

CHRISTMAS MAZE

Help Santa find the way through
to reach his sleigh

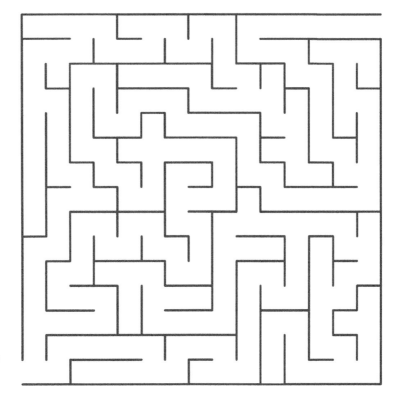

MERRY CHRISTMAS

WORD SEARCH

Find and circle the words.

M	T	R	D	B	Y	B	A	G	Y	T	A	R	T
R	E	I	N	D	E	E	R	N	S	E	L	O	M
U	R	B	I	K	N	R	A	H	D	O	D	L	I
T	C	E	L	E	B	R	A	T	E	G	N	H	S
R	E	C	H	R	I	S	T	M	A	S	H	A	T
X	Y	Z	D	U	L	O	R	H	A	U	A	G	L
H	O	L	I	B	A	U	B	L	E	I	N	D	E
U	X	G	B	R	A	E	T	Y	K	R	T	A	T
W	R	E	A	T	H	M	A	S	P	E	A	L	O
P	G	O	R	N	A	M	E	N	T	S	N	T	E
K	T	Y	O	S	T	O	C	K	I	N	G	L	M

- reindeer
- wreath
- bauble
- christmas
- stocking
- mistletoe
- celebrate
- ornaments

CHRISTMAS

Complete the dot to dot to reveal the Christmas image. Color once completed.

Christmas tree

COUNT AND COLOR

Count the objects and color the correct number.

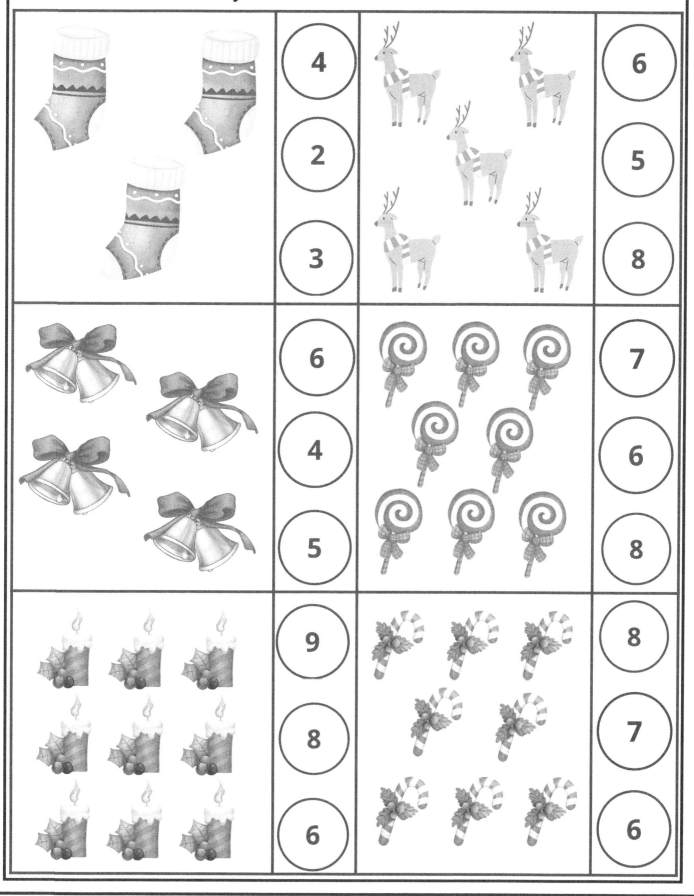

Christmas Word Search

Find the hidden Christmas words

J A N U A R Y N U R D C
H X E P N C L O C K A O
F M W H G R V F E T R U
I I Y T F A P O L U P N
R D E M I N U T E R A T
E N A T N T B H B K R D
W I R E I H A C R E T O
O G E N G A L D A Y Y W
R H R E S O L U T I O N
K T R A E I O O E R I S
S F A M F L O C R A F N
B R I N D A N C E N E L

MINUTE	DANCE	PARTY	CLOCK
CELEBRATE	MIDNIGHT	NEW YEAR	JANUARY
COUNTDOWN	FIREWORKS	RESOLUTION	BALLOON

Christmas
Ball

FIND THE SHADOW!

Draw a line from the object to the correct shadow.

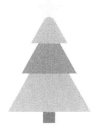

CHRISTMAS NUMBERS

Find the missing numbers and type in the circles.

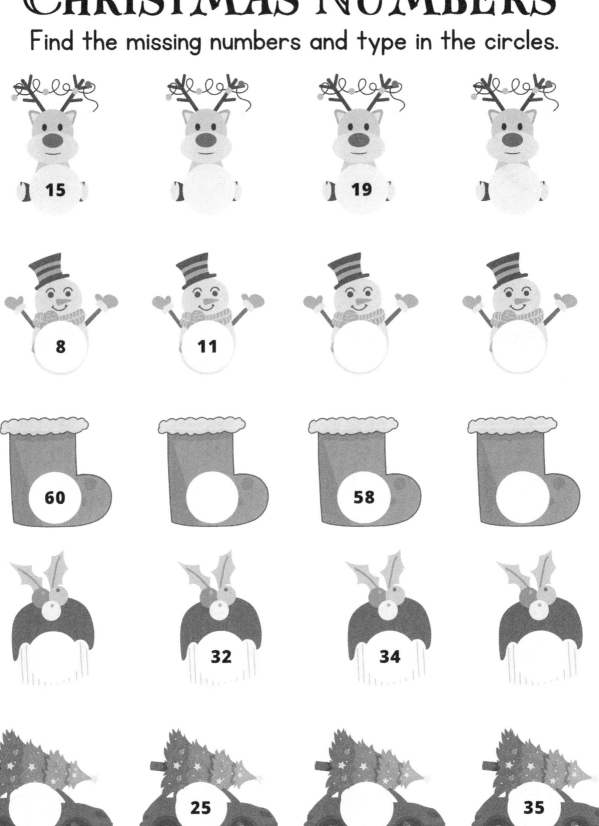

CHRISTMAS COORDINATES

Find the coordinates of the objects in the table,
write them in the field below.

← Columns →

	A	B	C	D	E	F	G	H	I
1						🎄			
2	🧦								⭐
3				🔮					
4								🏠	
5									🔴
6				NORTH POLE					
7							🦌		
8		🛷							
9					🍪				⛄

Rows

(**A** , **2**)   (..... , ...)   (..... , ...)   (..... , ...)   (..... , ...)   (..... , ...)
Column Row

(..... , ...)   (..... , ...)   (..... , ...)   (..... , ...)   (..... , ...)   (..... , ...)

SWEET ADDITIONS

Find the sum in each equation.
Write your answer after the equal sign.

🎄🎄🎄🎄🎄 + 🎄🎄🎄🎄🎄 =

🍭🍭🍭🍭🍭🍭 + **7** =

🛷🛷🛷🛷 🛷🛷🛷
🛷🛷🛷🛷 + 🛷🛷🛷
🛷🛷🛷🛷 =

❄❄❄❄❄ + ❄❄❄
❄❄❄❄❄ + ❄❄❄ =

6 + 2 + 3 =

Lots of
gifts

CHRISTMAS SUDOKU

Each row across and column down needs one of each image.
There can't be more than one image in any row across or column down.
Cut the pictures and paste them to complete Sudoku.

CHRISTMAS MAZE

Help the letter get to the North Pole

Its almost
midnight

CHRISTMAS NUMBERS

Find the missing numbers and type in the circles.

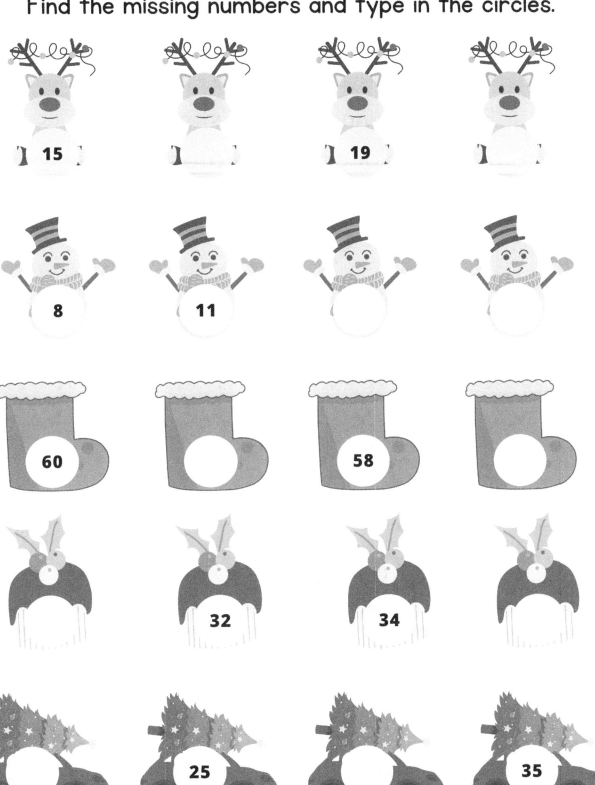

CHRISTMAS DECOR

Finish drawing the Christmas Tree.
Color and decorate it.

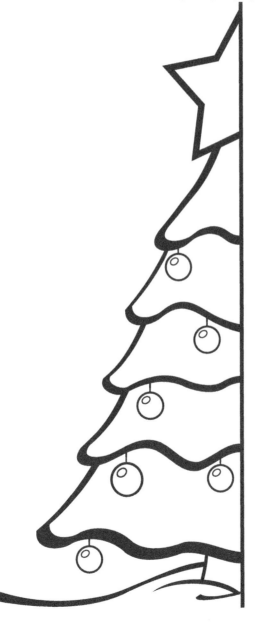

CHRISTMAS

Complete the dot to dot to reveal the Christmas image. Color once completed.

I Spy Christmas

Count the Christmas-themed items in the box and record
the sum in the spaces provided below.

Home
sweet home

Christmas Maze Game

Help Santa to find the way to the house.

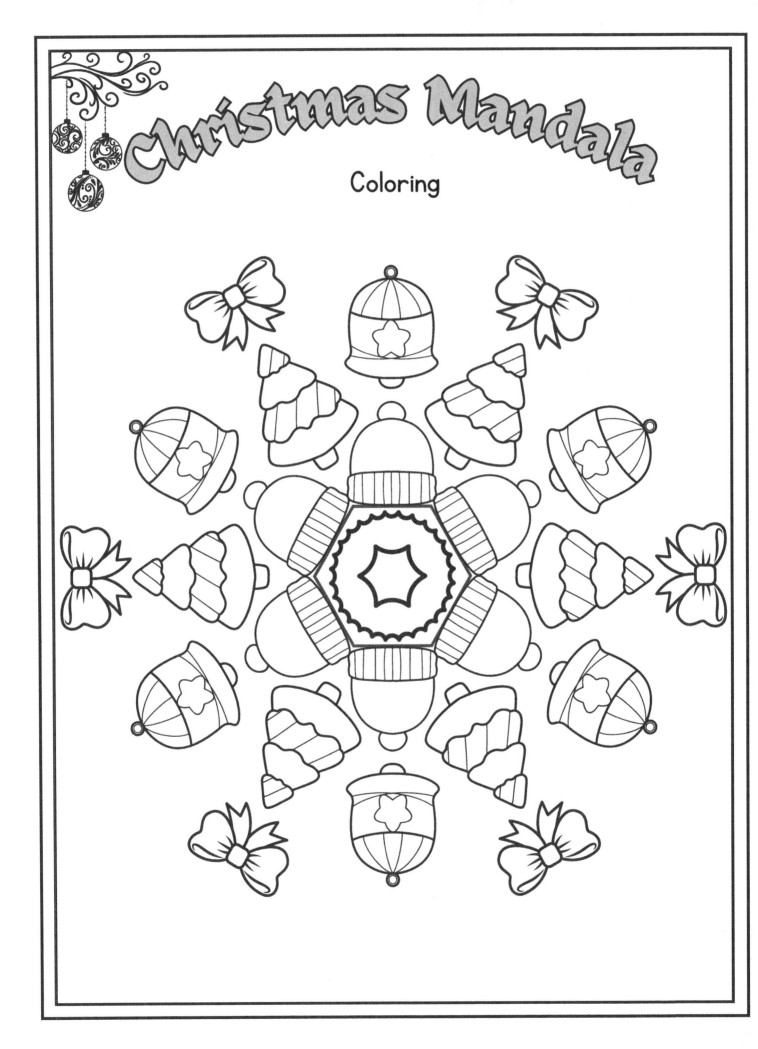

Christmas
candy

FIND THE SHADOW!

Draw a line from the object to the correct shadow.

CHRISTMAS COORDINATES

Find the coordinates of the objects in the table, write them in the field below.

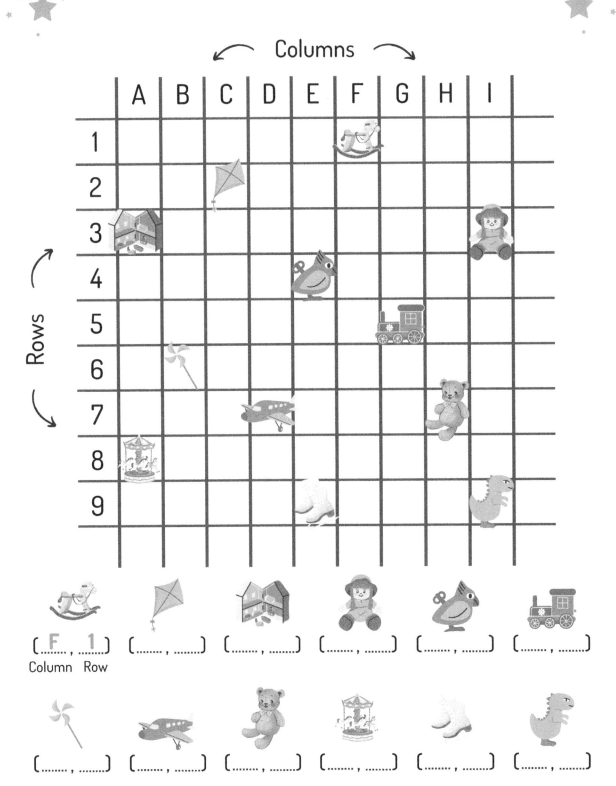

Columns

Rows

(F , 1)
Column Row

(...... , ...)

(...... , ...)

(...... , ...)

(...... , ...)

(...... , ...)

(...... , ...)

(...... , ...)

(...... , ...)

(...... , ...)

(...... , ...)

(...... , ...)

CHRISTMAS SUDOKU

Each row across and column down needs one of each image.
There can't be more than one image in any row across or column down.
Cut the pictures and paste them to complete Sudoku.

CHRISTMAS MAZE

Find your way to bring home
the Christmas tree!

Happy
snowman

WORD SEARCH

B C E F P A E L B C S Z
S N O W M A N B V A L K
H R F S M T R Y Q R E B
Y B U I T D R J S O I R
K G M T S N W E H L G X
S D R A C C E O E S H G
P U N Y C B L S T U D H
P T Y Z M I S K E U C Y
A R E E D N I E R R D G
S N R A Z Z S F M N P Z
U D Y Y B G S T A L S D
D G B K R D L C F M L K

| CANDY | CARDS | CAROLS | PRESENTS | HOLIDAY |

| REINDEER | SANTA | SLEIGH | SNOWMAN | TREE |

CHRISTMAS CODING

Examine the numbers corresponding to the toys.
Encode the passwords inside the circle with lines.

| 1 | 2 | 3 | 4 | 5 | 6 | 7 | 8 |

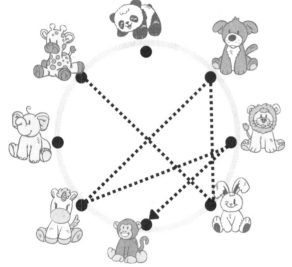

PASSWORD: 8-4-2-6-3-5

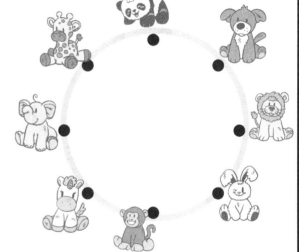

PASSWORD: 5-2-7-1-4-6

PASSWORD: 2-6-5-4-1-7

PASSWORD: 3-8-6-1-4-2

Light of Bethlehem

CHRISTMAS

Complete the dot to dot to reveal the Christmas image. Color once completed.

Help Santa find his way to Mrs Claus

MERRY CHRISTMAS!

FIND THE HIDDEN OBJECTS

I Spy Christmas

Count the Christmas-themed items in the box and record the sum in the spaces provided below.

Cold
penguin

Christmas words

Fill in the missing letters

L_NT__N

_AB_ JE_U_

L_TT_R
TO S_N_A

USI B_X

C_OI_

NUT_RA_KE_

C__RC_

S_EI_H

TE_D_ _EA_

_OL_Y
BE_R_ES

B_RD_O_SE

_UPC_K_

CHRISTMAS NUBERS

Find the missing numbers and type in the circles.

Forever
Christmas

WORD SEARCH

```
C O P V C O R N F L E P
A R I S N Y E K R U T R
L B E L L U M P I E G E
H A G I T E H G I E N S
T G R A N A I T C M I E
A S I U P D U G O P K N
E T H R C O E N H F C T
R O A B O R I E S C O Y
W T T R G A T H R R T A
S N O W F L A K E Y S M
```

SNOWFLAKE   SLEIGH   BELL
STAR   REINDEER   STOCKING
PRESENT   WREATH   ELF

SWEET SUBTRACTION

Find the difference in each equation.
Write your answer after the equal sign.

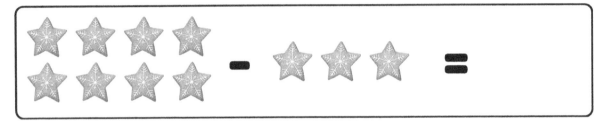

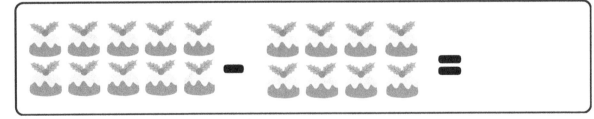

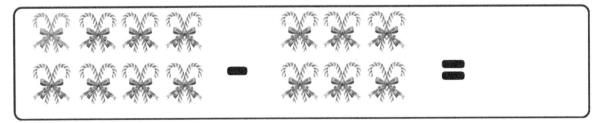

CHRISTMAS COORDINATES

Find the coordinates of the objects in the table,
write them in the field below.

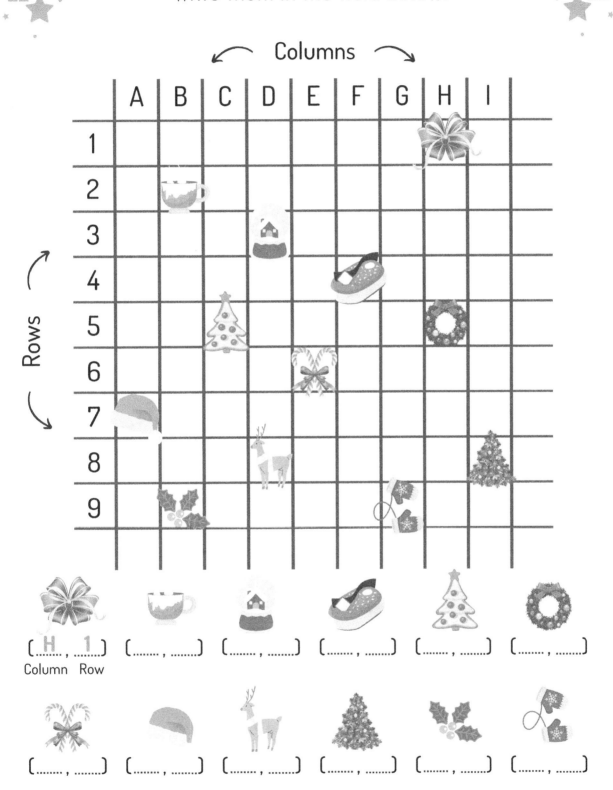

(H , 1)
Column Row

(...... , ...)   (...... , ...)   (...... , ...)   (...... , ...)   (...... , ...)

(...... , ...)   (...... , ...)   (...... , ...)   (...... , ...)   (...... , ...)   (...... , ...)

CHRISTMAS

Complete the dot to dot to reveal the Christmas image. Color once completed.

Seasons
greeting

CHRISTMAS SUDOKU

Each row across and column down needs one of each image.
There can't be more than one image in any row across or column down.
Cut the pictures and paste them to complete Sudoku.

CHRISTMAS MAZE

Find the way through to reach gifts to put them under the Christmas tree.

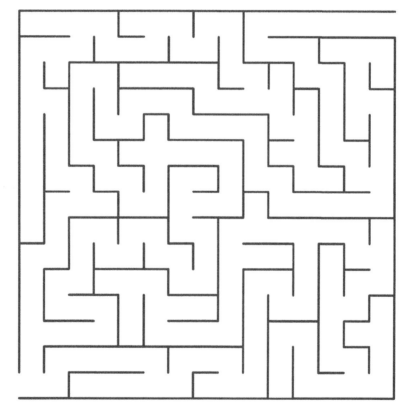

Cute little
horse

Christmas words

Fill in the missing letters

CH_IS_M_S T_EE

G__G_R M_N

C_RI_T_A_ SO_K

C_N_LE

_E_LS

R_BB_N

_IF_

C_ND_ _AN_

G_OM_

W_EAT_

_LEI_H

R_IN_E_R

CHRISTMAS

Complete the dot to dot to reveal the Christmas image. Color once completed.

CHRISTMAS COORDINATES

Find the coordinates of the objects in the table,
write them in the field below.

Columns

	A	B	C	D	E	F	G	H	I
1								🎁	
2		🏠							
3				🍭			✨		
4			🧁						🧤
5	🍎								
6		⛄				🔔			
7									
8			🧦						🍪
9							🕯		

Rows

(**D** , **3**)   (...... , ...)   (...... , ...)   (...... , ...)   (...... , ...)   (...... , ...)

Column Row

(...... , ...)   (...... , ...)   (...... , ...)   (...... , ...)   (...... , ...)   (...... , ...)

Christmas Mandala

Coloring

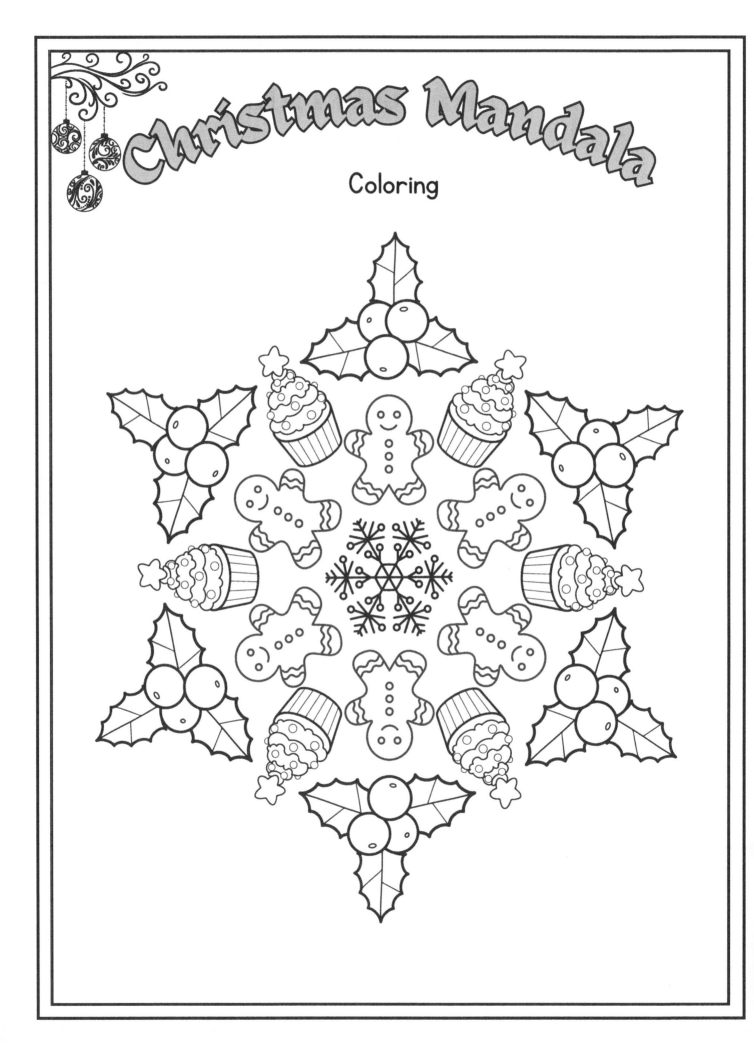

Advent candles

WORD SEARCH

```
G U E R U H M N B O R E Y T
A R E I N D E E R N R H N I
E E B O E D A E M D M J D Y
N L S L E I G H I S E M B S
M T F G I N G E R B R E A D
D A T N A S E A Y P R S M A
J I I N N O D S E E Y C M R
I G C S I N E N E G M D C U
N R I P R E S E N T S G N D
G D J R C H R I S T M A S O
L I N Y O A M I M L N R T L
E J M N C E G N Y H E D S F
I M N E N E N A M W O N S A
F I I I C A N D Y E E R E G
```

CANDY	PRESENTS	SANTA	GINGERBREAD
MERRY	REINDEER	SLEIGH	CHRISTMAS
ELF	SNOWMAN	JINGLE	RUDOLF

A-MAZE-ING CHRISTMAS

Help Santa find his sleigh!

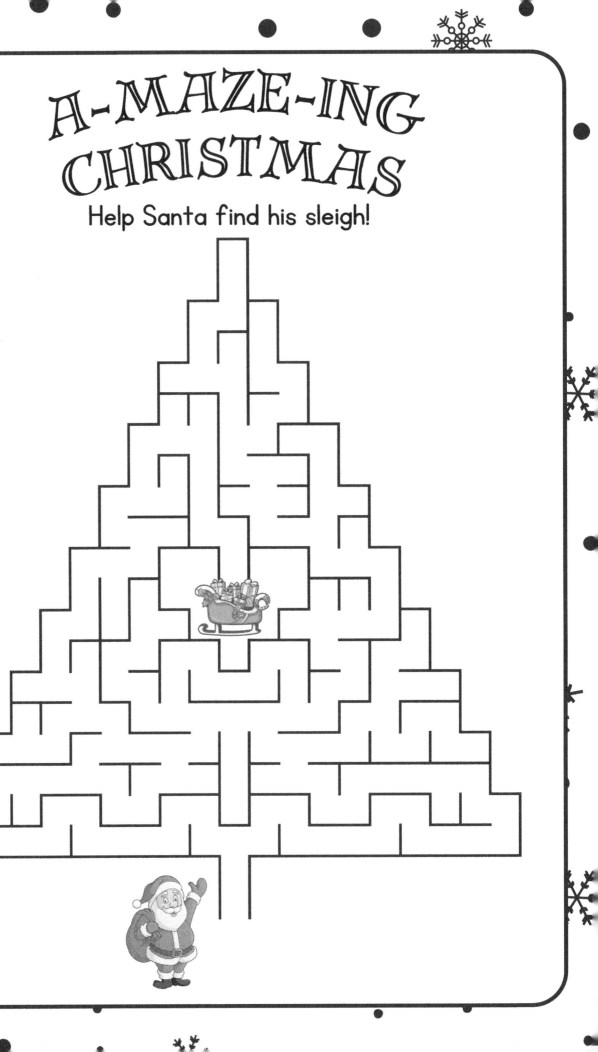

Christmas deliveries

CHRISTMAS VOCABULARY

Complete the words according to the numbers of the pictures.

1 S _ _ _ _ _ _ _ _ _

2 C _ _ _ _ _ _ _ _ T _ _ _

3 S _ _ _ _ C _ _ _ _

4 P _ _ _ _ _ _

5 S _ _ _ G _ _ _ _

6 C _ _ _ _ _ _

7 R _ _ _ _ _ _ _

8 M _ _ _ _ _

CHRISTMAS NUBERS

Find the missing numbers and type in the circles.

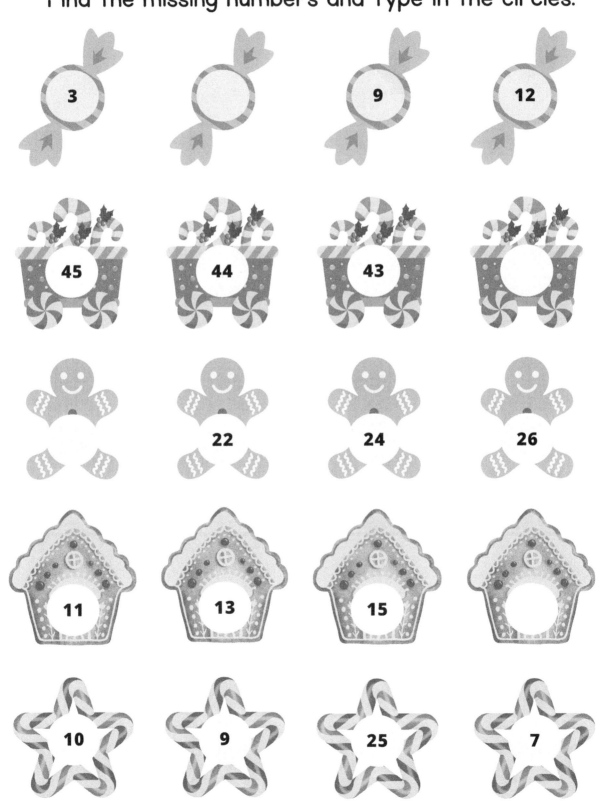

3		9	12
45	44	43	
	22	24	26
11	13	15	
10	9	25	7

CHRISTMAS SUBTRACTION

Find the difference in each equation. Write your answer after the equal sign.

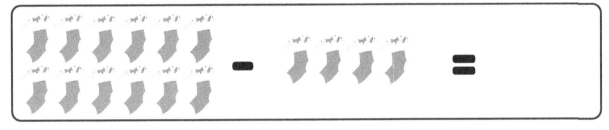

Christmas Coding

Examine the numbers corresponding to the Christmas decorations. Encode the passwords inside the circle with lines.

PASSWORD: 3-6-4-1-7-5

PASSWORD: 5-2-7-1-4-6

PASSWORD: 5-2-7-1-4-6

PASSWORD: 5-2-7-1-4-6

MERRY CHRISTMAS!

CHRISTMAS DECOR

Finish drawing the Christmas Tree.
Color and decorate it.

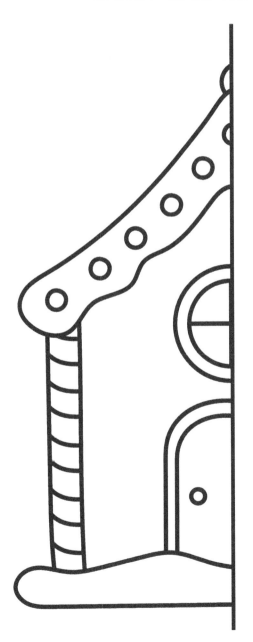

CHRISTMAS
WORD SCRAMBLE

Clues

Unscramble the Christmas vocabulary

erdniere	etre	raweth	gckiston
_____	_____	_____	_____

tamnrone	gegngo	nansmow	idpudng
_____	_____	_____	_____

neac	figt
_____	_____

I Spy Christmas

Count the Christmas cats in the box and record
the sum in the spaces provided below.

COLOURING IN

Dedicated to those who have chosen this book:

A big sincere

   With these activities, we hope you have enjoyed hours of fun and learning with your child, and that they have discovered the joy of learning new things.

   We publish our work exclusively on Amazon and we would appreciate it if you leave a positive review for this book: reviews are very useful and help us to succeed! Want to write a review for us? What did you like the most?
   And to thank us in an authentic way, send it to us too, in an email with the subject "Christmas" to

   redazione@polveredargento.it

and we will send you a PDF file with 30 adorable coloring pages, to print as many times as you want!
And if you are looking for novelties, original or completely personalized publications, for unique gift ideas, contact us any time!

This is our site:
   https://info81098.wixsite.com/passionelibri/books-in-english

Scan the QR Code above and find out how many books there are!

Happy Birthday Collection

There are so many other creations, you know? Many other children's books, even with a personalized name! Yes, with the name you want, on request!

With these creations, Grandma Ale would like all children to start loving books from an early age!

On the site, you will find many other creations, all customizable, even for mom and dad!

Look how beautiful our recipe notebooks are:

And remember: if you're looking for something more personal, for example for a recipe book with the name you want, as a splendid and original gift, contact us and we will give life to your very own creation!

Write to: redazione@polveredargento.it

We have a true **PASSION FOR BOOKS**!

ADVENT CALENDAR
Coloring Book

With Advent Calendar to color, a real 3D nativity scene, ready to be colored and cut out and more!!!

Keep an eye on this page:

https://info81098.wixsite.com/passionelibri/books-in-english

Made in the USA
Las Vegas, NV
09 December 2023

82346542R00063